CAMPANULA *vulgatior foliis Urtica vel major & asperior.* C.B.P.

G.D. Ehret pinxit.
1757

ampanula medium L.), with Drinker Moth (*Philudoria potatoria* L.). Body-colour on vellum, signed, 1757

In Bloom

CREATING AND LIVING WITH FLOWERS

Ngoc Minh Ngo

RIZZOLI
NEW YORK

New York Paris London Milan

"Everything is blooming most recklessly"
RAINER MARIA RILKE

Contents

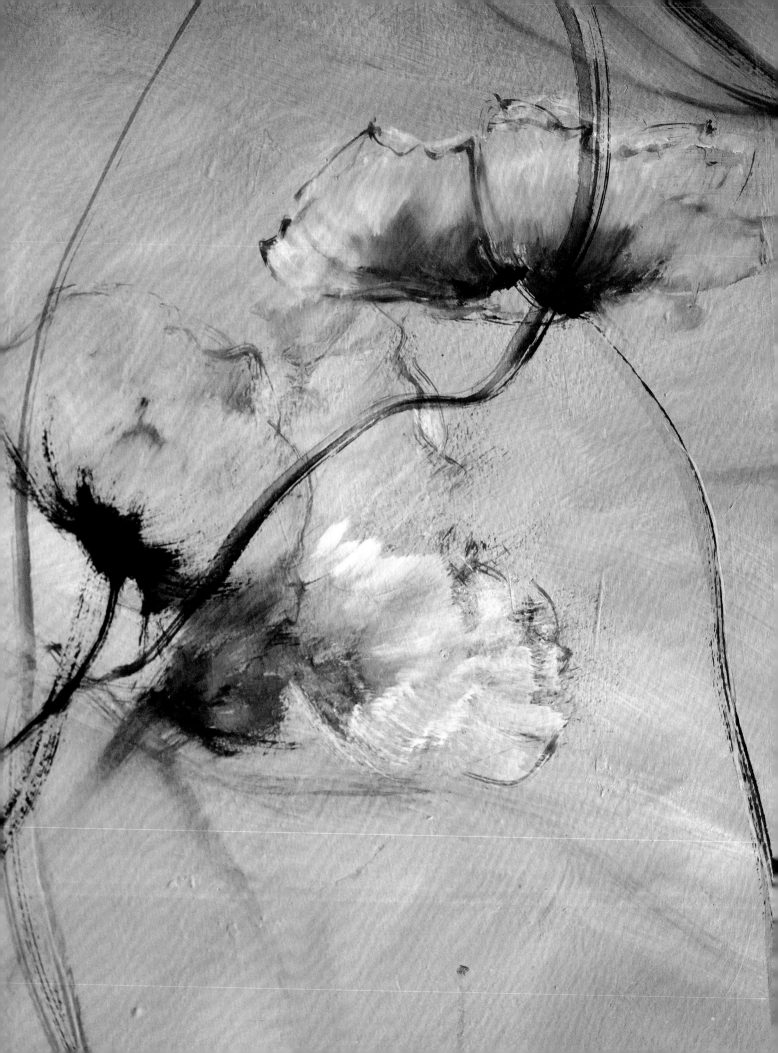

The Beauty of Flowers

THE WORLD IS FULL OF BEAUTY, and few things are more beautiful than flowers. For millennia, flowers have been weaving their way into the fabric of our lives, claiming a central place in the human experience. The first flowers appeared on Earth some 125 million years ago: nothing more than primitive versions of the water lily, unassuming and thriving on the edges of the Cretaceous lakes in the shadow of dinosaurs. These long lost pioneers made their way on land, eventually evolving into the infinite variety of complex and showy blossoms that fascinate and delight us today. We don't know when flowers first found their place in the lives of men, but vases unearthed from Mesopotamia have been found decorated with "garlands," leaving little doubt that prehistoric man was already seduced by their beauty. Like all civilizations before us—from the ancient Chinese and Egyptians to the Persians, Greeks, and Romans—we gather, grow, observe, admire, and record flowers for myriad reasons. We celebrate them in songs and poems. We love and mourn with flowers in hand. We borrow their loveliness to embellish our home, adorn our dresses, and grace our table.

The fugitive beauty of flowers has always had an intense resonance for us. The ancient Greeks held an extraordinary passion for flowers and found use for them in every aspect of their public and private lives. Flowers were offered at the altars of the gods, crowned the heads of youths, and decorated the gates of the city in times of rejoicing. Early Minoan vases were alive with palm trees, lilies, tulips, and reeds. Dazzling floral paintings decorated palace walls. In the Springtime Landscape Fresco on the Greek island of Santorini, mysterious red lilies rise out of a rocky landscape while swallows swoop in the sky. At the Knossos Palace, *Rosa pulverulenta*, a wild rose species with pine-scented leaves and abundant crimson hips that still grows today along the rocky shores of the Mediterranean, was painted alongside irises, just as it must have appeared 3,500 years ago. Pliny the Elder tells us the story of one of the first flower painters, Pausias from the ancient city of Sicyon on the Peloponnese. Young Pausias was in love with the gifted garland maker Glycera, whose floral wreaths he sought to imitate in paint. A friendly competition for the most beautiful creation of flowers formed between the young lovers until Pausias's painted blooms rivaled Glycera's real blossoms.

Like the Greeks, the Romans also had a fondness for flowers, sometimes to excess. Crowned in laurel wreaths, victorious generals and their armies paraded their spoils of wars through flowers-strewn streets, to be greeted with garlands thrown from windows and rooftops by the adoring crowd. While Zeus might have slept on a bed of saffron, lotus, and hyacinth, in imperial Rome a bed of rose petals was the height of luxury. Roses, sometimes imported from as far as Egypt, were also a must at every great banquet. In Emperor Nero's opulent rotating banquet hall, ivory panels on the ceiling slid back to shower blossoms and perfumes upon guests. Lesser mortals simply scattered flowers on the dining table, a practice continued until the Renaissance, when embroidered tablecloths replaced real blossoms, to be followed by printed blooms a few centuries later.

During the late fifteenth and early sixteenth centuries, exotic flowers from the fertile Tien Shan Mountains of Central Asia made their way into Europe via the Silk Road. Colorful fritillary, lily, hyacinth, anemone, crocus, iris, and tulip bulbs were tucked into bundles of silk and brought to Constantinople, the gateway to Western Europe, where they passed from merchants to nurserymen, from ambassadors to emperors, from botanists to gardeners, to populate the new botanic gardens in Pisa, Vienna, Leiden, Paris, and London. Noblemen built lavish private gardens to show off these botanical treasures. Flowers became subjects of scientific studies, and botanists and painters alike, with the use of the microscope, were able to contemplate the blooms' specific complexity and beauty as never before. Such artists as Leonardo da Vinci and Albrecht Dürer embraced the ideal of the Renaissance, an all-around learning founded on scientific curiosity and a close study of nature. Dürer's watercolors of irises, pansies, columbines, and other wildflowers were astonishingly lifelike and exquisitely rendered, an inspiration to the masters of Dutch flower paintings a century later. Meanwhile, flowers were all the rage at the court of Marie de' Medici, wife of King Henry IV of France. The Queen loved to surround herself with blossoms in her gardens, as well as in paintings and fine embroidery. The King's engraver and embroiderer, Pierre Vallet, dedicated to her his *florilegium*, one of the first flower books of its kind; its intricate flower images were in part to document the rare plants brought back from Spain and Guinea, and in part to provide new embroidery designs for the ladies at court.

It was under the patronage of another plant lover, the Empress Joséphine, that Pierre-Joseph Redouté, the "Raphael of flowers," did some of his finest work. Joséphine, Napoléon's first wife, bought the Château de Malmaison just outside of Paris with the ambition of creating "the most beautiful and curious garden in Europe," spending vast sums of money to build greenhouses and import plants from all over the world. Rare tulips were ordered from Holland, lilies brought from the Nile. A double white form of a Chinese Mountain Peony, hibiscus, phlox, dahlias, and many other exotic plants bloomed for the first time in France at Malmaison. In her luxuriant gardens, various species of magnolia from China and America grew alongside eucalypti and acacias from Australia, while fifty different species of pelargonium and heath from South Africa flourished in the greenhouses modeled on those at Kew Gardens. Joséphine, whose real name was Rose before Napoléon summarily changed it, had the most lasting impact on the culture of her namesake. She made it her goal to collect every species of rose then known, and Malmaison became the epicenter of the cultivation of roses. Napoléon even gave an order to the French Navy to search for plants or rose seeds on any ships seized at sea. New china roses were given safe passage from England to Malmaison by the British Admiralty despite the naval blockade at the time. French growers were inspired to hybridize new cultivars for the empress, some of which are still grown today by rose lovers all over the world.

To record her treasured plant collection at Malmaison, Joséphine turned to Redouté, who had been the flower painter and drawing master of Marie-Antoinette. With their precise botanical details rendered thrillingly realistic, Redouté's images of plants and flowers remain unsurpassed in their three-dimensionality and the singular beauty that made so many pre-eminent botanists at the time rely on his talents. Today Redouté is celebrated for his best-known publication, *Les Roses*, begun at the instigation of Joséphine and published after her death. During her lifetime, Redouté published several volumes that celebrate the flora of Malmaison, copies of which were bought by Joséphine and Napoléon to stock their library as well as to give as official presents. But Redouté's botanical illustrations were appreciated beyond the library at Malmaison: a series of watercolors decorated the empress's bedroom, and two great dessert services were produced for her based on his engravings.

In eighteenth-century England, the quest to record the beauty of plants and flowers, many of which were brought back from the New World by such intrepid plant hunters as Sir Joseph Banks, led Mary Delany to create a new art form. At the grand age of seventy-two, Mrs. Delany, a skilled painter and embroiderer, made the first of nearly one thousand "paper mosaicks"—inventive painted-paper collages of flowers at once visually exquisite and botanically precise—weaving together the different threads of her life: gardening, botany, painting, and a deep love for the beauty of flowers. Her art was rooted in the science of botany, much like the unique collection of glass flowers that the father and son German glassmakers Leopold and Rudolph Blaschka made for the Harvard Botanical Museum a century later. Fifty years in the making, these fragile beauties—stunningly vivid models of more than 850 plant species—offer some of the finest observations of nature, crystallized through an unparalleled mastery of the art of glassmaking.

For thousands of years, we have found inspiration in the enduring appeal of flowers, refashioning them in every possible guise, yet as the works of the artists in this book can attest, we remain as spellbound by their charm as Pausias was with Glycera's blooms. Our technology-fueled world has only increased our craving to connect with nature, and the beauty of the botanical realm continues to be the perfect foil for the magic of the human imagination. Shaped by our desire, flowers carry our human history in their very being: the footprints of our quest for knowledge and adventure, a repository of our notions and meanings. Flowers will always exert their grip on us, as long as our human yearning for beauty remains. Think of Mondrian's elegiac chrysanthemums, Fantin-Latour's voluptuous roses, Van Gogh's joyous sunflowers, Dürer's earthy columbines, the sensuous peonies in Chinese silk paintings, the elegant tulips on Iznik pottery, or the rich flowery meadows that spring up on medieval tapestries and William Morris's wallpapers. Gaze into a flower, and inscribed in its bewildering patterns are intimations of nature's duality: its creative force and its rapid dissolution. Like a Robert Frost poem that begins in delight and ends in wisdom, flowers seduce us with their piercing beauty but they also have much to teach us about the impermanent nature of life. On the last day of his life, the painter Pierre-Auguste Renoir, already weakened by months of ill health, asked for his paint box and brushes and began to paint a bouquet of anemones that Nénette, the maidservant, had picked for him in the garden. For several hours, he lost himself in the flowers and forgot his pain. As he finished and handed over his brushes, Renoir spoke his last words: "*Je crois que je commence à y comprendre quelque chose.*"*

*"I think that I am beginning to understand something about it."

Untamed Bouquets

SARAH RYHANEN   *Brooklyn & Esperance, New York*

SARAH RYHANEN CAN CLEARLY REMEMBER THE MOMENT she discovered the mysterious power of flowers. For her twenty-fifth birthday, her partner, Eric Famisan, presented her with an unusual bouquet of black dahlias. "Being given flowers made me feel very special, and black dahlias, which I had never seen before, are so sexy and alluring. I was touched by the sentiment of the gesture as well as the beauty of those velvety dahlias," recalls Sarah. It didn't matter that the flowers died the very next day; "their work had already been done." The power of the dahlias was revelatory and ignited her passionate love affair with flowers. Having always been an artist—she did performance art in college and was working at the time as an assistant curator in a New York gallery—Sarah finally found her true medium. Soon she began to haunt the flower market, asking questions and learning as much as she could about flowers. Before long, she and Eric were running their shop, Saipua (from the Finnish word for soap, *saippua)*, in the Red Hook neighborhood of Brooklyn, selling an unusual combination of olive-oil soaps made by her mother and wildly beautiful flower arrangements by Sarah.

Saipua's bouquets are never conventional, beginning with a palette that gravitates toward what Sarah calls "the muddy, in-between colors," like mauve, pale blush (neither white nor pink), and brown. Rejecting the standard-issue tight dome-shaped bouquets, she favors loose, naturalistic compositions, teasing out the singular beauty of each individual blossom, mixing peonies or garden roses with wild vines and foliage that look like they had been picked from abandoned fields and roadsides. Her signature arrangements came to define a certain Brooklyn aesthetic in the floral art, spawning imitators as far as Korea and Japan, but Sarah's work remains inimitably original—seemingly wild and effortless, as though she had casually gathered everything from the field, yet thoughtfully sculptural and inventive, and undeniably breathtaking.

The quest for more "natural" looking blooms, not the hothouse-grown varieties completely devoid of character that were the staple of the flower market after the economy crashed in 2008, led Sarah and Eric to start growing their own flowers on a farm some four hours outside of New York City. World's End, named for a favorite T. C. Boyle novel, is a picture of bucolic beauty, complete with a nineteenth-century white farmhouse, a lily-covered pond, twenty acres of cleared fields with rows of flowers and grazing Icelandic sheep, and a weathered barn that's been painstakingly restored. The reality of life on the farm is not always so picturesque—punishingly harsh winters, challenging soil conditions, and demanding physical work—but the rewards are manifold. "The life lesson of the farm is patience," muses Sarah, "a magnolia tree planted today will be magnificent in thirty-five years." Meanwhile, she feels like "the luckiest flower arranger in the world during peak season," selecting exactly what she wants for her bouquets from the field, picking not just her favorite brown bearded irises, black hellebores, and rare martagon lilies, to name a few, but also "the branches of juneberry that are delightfully crooked, the coral bell leaves that are mottled and speckled with brown spots, and the wild grapevine and native berries that grow everywhere." World's End has also fed Sarah's passion for photography, another means to communicate her love for flowers. Her widely read blog is a platform for both her frank, witty, and at times heartbreaking musings on life at the farm, and her evocative images of flowers. A typical post describes her struggle with various woes on the farm, including a herd of sick sheep and obstinate weeds threatening to obliterate the flower field, with detours to a favorite YouTube music video ("We are the World") and her indignation at the cultural subjugation of women, and ends with her gladness to be living her dream, all interspersed with astonishingly beautiful photographs of her campanula.

Sarah has ambitious plans for World's End, which she envisions as a center for botanical arts, a place of exchange where she can share all that she has learned from being a flower and sheep farmer and foster experiences for some of her "core audience," young people who read the blog and "feel some emotional connection" to what she does. "I want to give these young people the opportunity to see how we grow flowers and arrange them, to see how the sheep live, how they are milked and then how cheese is made. But more importantly, how these things intersect and benefit each other, how the sheep graze on the flower fields that are spent, fertilizing them, for example." Her passion is infectious, and she is generous with her knowledge and time. Young interns flock to World's End from around the country to work on the fields and glean her techniques in flower arranging.

In Sarah's artful hands, the emotional power of flowers is made exquisitely palpable. Like the best of the seventeenth-century *vanitas* flower still-life paintings, Sarah's arrangements lay bare the poignancy of flowers, being at once so vivacious and so quick to fall. "I love to capture flowers in an arrangement when they are teetering on the edge of dying, that moment when they are most beautiful but also most vulnerable." That their beauty could be shattered in a moment makes it all the more piercing. "The most beautiful flowers are often the most fleeting." The most fragrant roses wilt in minutes, but they offer an unforgettably sensual experience. At their best, flowers teach you "to live in the moment, and then to let go."

Paper Petals

LIVIA CETTI   *Bronx, New York*

LIVIA CETTI HAS BEEN MAKING FLOWERS in one form or another for as long as she can remember. Growing up in the mountain north of Santa Barbara with artistic parents—her father made pottery while her mother painted, sewed, and did printmaking—Livia had the run of the family's forty-acre land, exploring all kinds of plant life. She spent long hours working in her father's garden, where they grew cacti and succulents. At age five, she made her first flower boutonnière, and through high school, and later, art school in San Francisco, she worked with some of the best florists. In New York, Livia helped a friend's photographer boyfriend on a shoot and soon found herself in demand as a floral stylist. She turned to making paper flowers when a client requested an artificial bloom as a cake topper for a Caribbean wedding. Her first paper flower, a hibiscus, remains a popular item in her ever-expanding repertoire, showing up in ad campaigns for Kate Spade and others. For a state dinner for South Korea at the White House, Livia made more than two hundred paper specimens of this tropical beauty.

These days, while not styling flowers for photo shoots or designing floral arrangements for special events, Livia can be found making her magical paper blossoms in the studio at the farmhouse she shares with her husband and two boys in the Bronx, New York. While she loves working with real flowers, she's found paper to be the perfect medium in which to express her passion for their beauty. What makes her work unique is the way she uses paper, and the time she devotes to preparing it. For the petals, her preference is tissue paper, which she bleaches, dyes, and sometimes paints meticulously to get the desired color gradation effects of real blooms. With each piece of hand-dyed paper, the result is different and thereby suggests what kind of flower it should be. The paper is then cut by hand, crimped, and fringed to resemble petals. For the foliage, Livia uses the matte Canson paper, cutting each individual leaf by hand, creasing and folding so that no two leaves look alike. Some foliage, like that of geraniums, requires additional painting with gouache to effect stripes and spots. For flowering quince and cherry blossoms, she uses real branches, adding her paper buds in place of real ones. Employing techniques similar to those used by milliners to assemble silk flowers, Livia puts the disparate pieces together with floral wire and tape. The resulting blossoms are astonishingly beautiful, whimsical, and poetic, all in equal parts.

Never wanting to make the same thing twice, Livia is constantly experimenting with new forms, different methods of dyeing and painting, and new paper colors. She has created eight different forms of roses, and she is constantly refining her dahlias, bleeding hearts, and tulips, among others. The starting point of every new flower is the question of how to translate into paper what she likes most about that particular genus. This conundrum can stay in her mind for a long time until she finds the right material among the stacks of paper that she bleaches, dyes, and paints constantly. It has to be in the right tone and gradation of color for the beauty of a particular flower to come to life. Livia has tackled every form of flower, from the simple poppy to the wispy honeysuckle to the elaborately sculptural foxglove. While she finds beauty in most flowers, delicate, bell-shaped, and simple blossoms like fritillaries, poppies, and camellias are closest to her heart.

Livia's work, rooted in the long tradition of artificial flower making, is a nod to the disappearing craft of millinery. Her inspiration comes from all forms of flowers, from the African floral headpieces by the Surma and Munsi tribes to her large collection of vintage flowers in beads, wax, silk, porcelain, and paper. Her floral tributes, though often simplified and highly stylized, still retain the essence that makes them immediately identifiable. She might like to play with the scale of flowers, at times making them far larger than life, but her intimate knowledge of each individual genus and their essential characteristics comes through in her interpretations. Her extraordinary blooms have the texture, movement, and delicateness of the real things. Each of her paper flowers speaks of her time spent in the garden, observing real ones. Her small but rambling garden is a plant lover's haven, where bearded irises, peonies, and bleeding hearts jostle for space next to columbines, geraniums, and cascading branches of spirea. There is always an abundance of blooms or interesting foliage for Livia to cut and make her signature wild arrangements for the house all year round. She is happiest in her studio, fashioning flowers out of her exquisitely dyed paper, or lost in her garden, putting yet more plants in the ground and watching the flowers grow.

44

Ruth Sterling Frost. Lucca 1951

The Poetry of Gardens

MIRANDA BROOKS   *Brooklyn & Long Island, New York*

EVER SINCE ADAM AND EVE WERE EXPELLED FROM THE GARDEN OF EDEN, men and women in different times and places have strived to create their own version of Eden. Earthly gardens come in all sizes, from great monuments to humble city allotments—places in which we have invested all kinds of meanings and aspects of our human existence. The Persians called their gardens *pairi-daeza*, which was later shortened to *paradiz*, our word for paradise. The ancient Chinese cultivated gardens that were a kind of microcosm of the universe, the haunts of poets and philosophers as much as birds and flowering trees. For the humble cottage gardener, a garden is simply a place to grow flowers. For Miranda Brooks, every great garden encompasses all these elements, as places of retreat as well as immersion, with intimations of paradise, heady with fragrance, silken petals, flights of butterflies and birdsong, as well as an extraordinary sense of peace, like a friend's garden in the south of Spain that she fell deeply in love with when she was seventeen. "It was made around a twelfth-century Moorish tower and rill, each cobble laid with skill and imagination, alive with the sound of water in rills and fountains, delicious scents and quiet places."

As a sought-after landscape designer with projects spreading from Somerset to Sag Harbor and Saint-Tropez, Miranda has created lush and romantic gardens that connect the house to the wider landscape, blending seamlessly man and nature, the cultivated and the untamed. "There might be small moments of drama, but primarily the transition of the garden areas to the surrounds is a blurred one. On a sensory level, scent and the edible element follow fast on the heels of the visual," says Miranda on the guiding principle behind her designs. Lemon-scented auriculas, musky sweet peas, and perfumed damask roses may thrill visitors to her gardens, but what sets them apart most of all is a distinct sense of place that reflects their many layers of meaning acquired either through her love of the land or the relationship with the person for whom the garden is created. The many gardens she creates become "places that I love and nurture," she says, "and in the best of moments an interior landscape that comes to fruition."

Miranda's love of gardens had its roots in her idyllic childhood in England. Born in Lancashire, she spent her first years in the country, playing in the family's wild orchard surrounded by a stream. "Lancashire has delicious black soil, and everything grows well: raspberries, potatoes, and of course, peas," recalls Miranda. "My strongest childhood memories are of nature as both an escape and a private idyllic symbiotic world, gamboling in the orchard, hiding in the bracken, or playing my recorder to my peas to help them grow. My father built a long ha-ha separating the ponies from the lawn and I spent many happy hours podding peas on that wall."

While her most personal gardens are deeply informed by her English upbringing, from the thyme and dianthus and dog-roses and honeysuckle combinations of Elizabethan gardens to the flora in Shakespeare's verses, she is equally adept evoking the same poetry in California or the Mediterranean using plants adapted for the local habitat. "It's about creating the same atmosphere using a different vocabulary," explains Miranda. On a visit to Kyoto, she fell in love with the sight of the remnants of persimmon fruits clinging to a tangle of bare branches, glowing in the landscape, which led her to plant persimmons against deciduous trees in a project in Los Angeles to create that moment of color in the barren months. Another winter tableau she conjures for a glade in the same garden is a carpet of fallen red blooms under the camellia trees. Every garden she creates is finely tuned to the rhythm of the seasons, from the first burst of blossoms in early spring through the explosion of flowers and scents in mid-summer to the mellowing of autumn and the stark beauty of winter.

Miranda's love of plants underlines these lyrical moments in the garden. While studying art history at the Courtauld Institute, she spent every weekend planting trees in the country. "The process of seeding and watching things grow is fascinating," says Miranda. "Every season brings new loves. Spring flowers like snowdrops and cowslips seem particularly brave, and it's such a thrill to see them." In late summer, she is enchanted by "*Clematis paniculata*, with its fluffiness and delicious scent, and the freshness and small buds of *Rosa* 'Cecile Brunner'." In winter, the extraordinary scent of *Daphne odorata* is another favorite.

In the Brooklyn home that she shares with her husband, Bastien Halard, and their two daughters, Miranda's passion for all things botanical pervades every room. "I always have flowers or branches in the house or it feels static," she says, echoing Vita Sackville-West's dictum that no room is ever complete without flowers. Flowering bulbs are brought in from the garden to herald the spring. Scented geraniums, grown in her small rooftop greenhouse, spill their fragrant leaves over the kitchen counter. In winter, branches of witch hazel are cut from the country to unfurl their perfumed spidery blooms in the bedroom. "Right now colchicums have breakfast with us. I chop and make tea next to dark red dahlias, and crab-apple branches are almost spilling into my bath," exclaims Miranda happily as the gentle autumn light slants through her windows. As the Chinese proverb goes, "If you want to be happy for a lifetime, plant a garden."

Memory of Nature

RACHEL DEIN   *London, England*

IN THE LIGHT-FILLED ATTIC STUDIO AT HER NORTH LONDON HOME, the artist Rachel Dein gently peels back a clay mold to reveal a plaster cast of flowers in amazing details and extraordinary beauty. The representation of nature has been the province of artists since the late Minoan painters and potters decorated palace walls and pottery with lilies, saffron, and other flowers thousands of years ago. Rachel's work evolved from the old tradition of nature printing, the technique of using the surface of a natural object to make a print. Leonardo da Vinci described the process in his *Codice Atlantico* of 1508, illustrating with a singular print of a sage leaf, its stem, mid-rib, veins, and curved edge standing out in vivid details. Early botanists used nature printing to record the plants they collected and to share information about new discoveries in faraway places. In the nineteenth century a young British printer named Henry Bradbury, borrowing techniques developed by the Austrian printer Alois Auer, published his most famous book, *The Ferns of Great Britain and Ireland.* Auer's innovative technique involved pressing the plants onto a thin, soft lead plate to make an *intaglio* impression. The fine grooves in the lead hold the ink, which is then transferred onto paper through a press. In the resulting images, fine botanical details are meticulously rendered with a slightly raised texture, bringing them alive on the page.

In a similar vein, Rachel Dein makes plaster casts of plants and flowers that record all their texture, pattern, and delicacy in exquisite details. Her composition can be as simple as a single stem or as complex as a field of wildflowers, leaves, and grasses. Pendulous bleeding hearts, curly fiddleheads of ferns, and wispy poppies are some of her favorite flowers to cast. There is a memorial as well as a celebratory quality to these simple tiles and panels, for they preserve a fleeting moment of glory long after the plants have faded and died. They reflect Rachel's interest in nature, its transience and tenacity. At art school, Rachel found her voice when she drew on a childhood memory of throwing a handful of melon seeds down the bathroom sink, only to discover, some weeks later, plants growing up through the overflow. "It seemed to encapsulate everything I wanted to express. It showed me how tough and tenacious nature is, which I found comforting," she says. It was a lesson that she applied to her life as well as her art, helping her cope with the serious illness of a loved one.

Combining her fascination with plants and sculpture—the works of Rodin and Andy Goldsworthy are her favorites—Rachel's floral castings are tactile and sculptural. Her method, adapted from a glass-casting technique learned in college, is deceptively simple. Flowers and foliage are arranged and pressed onto wet clay. A wooden frame is then placed on the clay and the plaster is poured in and allowed to set. The magical moment comes when Rachel lifts the clay mold to reveal the plants in their plaster incarnation. It is as if the real plants are enfolded within the plaster casting. The movement of a stem, the fragile fold of a petal, the veins on a leaf—every detail is caught and held in poetic suspension. The physicality of the plants is transferred onto the plaster, every graceful line of a stem or curve of a petal inviting the impulse to touch as much as to look at them.

Whether in small tiles with a single flower portrait or large panels that suggest an entire garden full of blooms, Rachel's botanical castings reflect her desire to capture the ephemeral. They track the progress of the seasons, marking the plants at the moment when they are most alive. Leeched of all colors and their flesh rendered in white plaster, the flowers are transformed, lending their gracefulness to something entirely new, at once a faithful imprint and an abstraction of themselves. With a tinge of sepia, the castings recall the slightly out-of-this-world look of platinum photographic prints brought into the third dimension. As light casts shadows on the relief, the plants take on an ethereal form, a haunting memory of their natural selves that have withered and vanished. Like a fossil of long forgotten plants, each plaque is a ghostly vestige of time, an act of remembering: a summer day in the garden, a perfect magnolia at its peak, or the first daffodils in spring. Relieved of their perishable forms and given permanence in white plaster, the floral castings carry with them forever the emotional impact of beauty. It is as if Rachel has distilled the flowers' essence into her tiles, each one the memory of nature itself.

A Thousand and One Flowers

UMBERTO PASTI   *Tangier & Rohuna, Morocco*

IN HIS BOOK *Le Bonheur du Crapaud*, the Italian writer and horticulturalist Umberto Pasti writes an impassioned elegy for the iris of Tangier, *Iris tingitana*. He tells us that at one time this iris species could be found everywhere in its native city, arranged in vases on restaurant tables and shop counters, in laundry windows and hotel rooms, and at the sellers of pop music. They also adorned the living rooms of the modernist villas in the city's California quarter, the apartments in the once-seedy neighborhood of M'sallah, and the bazaars in Soco Chico. In the cafés on the boulevard, old men sitting in front of their habitual mint tea wore them as boutonnières. "Hung from rearview car mirrors, next to a miniature plastic Koran, they evoked the era where families went for strolls around the bays and in forests on the backs of mules." When Umberto first arrived in Tangier in the early 1980s, *Iris tingitana* grew wild all over the city, carpeting immense fields from the southwest to the east, solid masses of purple bordering the old airport. His first encounter with the flower was a revelation. High above the Strait of Gibraltar, a sea of tall purple irises stretched out for miles in front of him and his partner, Stephan Janson. "Two oceans: one green, purple, and light blue, the other green, purple, and dark blue." Millions of irises: "each one observed up close gives the impression of being as rare as a unicorn even while it's standing next to hundreds of other identical flowers." Umberto discerns in the beauty of these irises the raw sensuality of the Berbers, the obsessive mysticism of the Idrisid Sufis fleeing Mecca and making their way to Tangier, and the desperate vitality of the Banu Hilal tribes that debarked on the shores of North Africa after long years of their exodus from the Arabic peninsula. Through a single flower, he could glimpse a thousand years of history, a world even more alive than reality.

Since that momentous voyage to the shores of Tangier, Umberto has made a magical home in the city for himself and Stephan, filled with wondrous flowers and his vast collection of Islamic tiles, another obsession since childhood. In thirty years, he has cultivated his garden and his passion for the botanical treasures of Tangier, delving into their colorful history. Once, outside the southern town Tzrout, he was surprised to come upon a specimen of the double narcissus, *N. telamonius plenus*. Introduced in England in 1620 by a Dutchman named Vincent Sion, it was much prized by the great botanists of the time, including John Tradescant the Younger, who planted it in his garden on the Thames and called it the Great Rose Daffodil, its flowers being as "double as a Provence Rose," as described by the great botanist John Parkinson. How such a flower found itself in the forgotten fields of southern Morocco was a mystery that haunted Umberto. The peasants of Tzrout insisted that it had always grown there, and the old people called it *Narcisse de l'Anglais* (the Englishman's Narcissus). The mysterious Englishman's identity eluded him until one day, an old man in a café casually told him that the English owner of the narcissus in question was the prisoner of "the generous *sherif* of Djebala"—the mountain chief Raisuni who once kidnapped and imprisoned his friend, the English journalist Walter Harris, for ransom. Harris had come to Morocco in 1887 at the age of nineteen and lived much of his life in a villa he built close to Tangier Bay and some three miles east of the city walls. Fluent in French, Spanish, and Arabic, he traveled freely to many parts of the country that were off-limits to foreigners at the time, forming unlikely friendships with both rebels like Raisuni and the sultans of Morocco. His imprisonment in Tzrout was brief—he was released in a prisoner exchange—but for many long years afterward, Harris came back repeatedly to his former jailer and lifelong friend, bringing the English-bred double narcissus from his garden in Tangier.

For Umberto, the rich history of Morocco is inscribed in the country's wildflowers. They are the portals through which the worlds of the past can be reached. In the last decade, rapid development has diminished their habitat, the fields of wildflowers around Tangier disappearing one by one, taking with them not only their beauty, but also the many stories that they carry with them. The once ubiquitous *Iris tingitana* has become increasingly rare. The sea of irises that captivated Umberto on his first visit to Tangier has completely vanished. Determined to stem the tide of destruction on the wildflowers of Morocco, Umberto has created an exceptional garden on the hills of Rohuna, a small village outside of Tangier, as a haven for these endangered beauties. Having transplanted there thousands of flowers rescued from construction sites, he plans to do much more. For gardeners like himself, "paradise doesn't exist elsewhere; it is here. It's called the world." To preserve these wildflowers is nothing less than a fight against the diminution of the world.

Painted Blossoms

CLAIRE BASLER   *Echassières, France*

TO BRING THE OUTSIDE INDOORS is an old ambition of architecture, and the painter Claire Basler does it brilliantly. She lives and works in an enchanting thirteenth-century château surrounded by eighty acres of woodlands and meadows that provide the perfect setting and inspiration for her paintings. At the heart of Claire's work is the observation of nature and the celebration of its vitality, its force, and its sensuality. The strength of nature is nowhere more evident than in Claire's favorite tree on the property, an ancient cedar that stands alone, rising out of the woods like a cathedral, its massive trunk looking like a dozen big trees tied together. It's a majestic, beautiful tree, reminiscent of the giant redwoods of California, a formidable presence that dwarfs all the other trees and stands immutable through rain, wind, and snow, season after season. Claire is also drawn to the fragile side of nature, the precarious beauty of flowers. She loves all flowers—peonies, poppies, irises, delphiniums, daisies, nasturtiums, roses, lilies, Queen Anne's lace, buttercups—and they appear in abundance on her canvases and on the walls of her magical home.

Château de Beauvoir is a place of singular beauty. The presence of nature permeates the property in different guises and layers: in the ever-changing landscape, in the wildly arranged flowers and branches that practically burst out of the rooms, and on the painted floral scenes that cover the walls in every direction. Her art, inspired by nature, creates a space where painted and real blossoms comingle and blend together seamlessly, where the landscape surrounding the château is experienced in multiple dimensions. The woodlands and the meadows are brought inside—both literally, through the cut branches and flowers, and figuratively, through the paintings—and transformed by her imagination to reappear on the walls in different moods, sometimes dramatic, almost operatic, other times quiet and serene, but always spectacular. To sleep among her larger-than-life poppies is like being in a fabulous dream. To walk along the long *enfilade* where the painted rooms unfold, each one a different landscape inhabited by different species of flowers, is to be reminded of the beauty of nature, its grandeur and frailty exquisitely illustrated.

This duality of strength and vulnerability is embodied in the place itself. The château had long been uninhabited when Claire found it. Both the land and the building had suffered from many years of neglect, but that did not deter Claire, who once made her home in an old ironworks factory, or her partner, Pierre Imhof, who, like all sailors, seems capable of fixing anything. Château de Beauvoir gave Claire the chance to create a world of her own. The expansiveness and richness of the land—dense woods thick with old trees and blooming rhododendrons in spring, large meadows colored with wildflowers in summer, and a garden that needs tending—feed Claire's love of nature, while the endless rooms, some in a state of disrepair, provide the blank canvases that she needs. The former *orangerie*, with light flooding through it in all seasons, makes the perfect painting studio. To restore the overgrown woodland, Pierre had to trim many of the trees, at times removing entire specimens that were ailing and crowding out healthier ones. The branches were hauled into the studio as decoration, and they've stayed there for years, creating a small forest at one end of the large room. At the other end, used glass yogurt jars holding Claire's mixed paint colors line up on the wall cabinets, a kaleidoscope of hues that comprise her ever-expanding palette. She divides her time between painting on canvas for gallery shows and painting the rooms of the château. It is the latter that she enjoys the most. Claire approaches the wall paintings with complete spontaneity—no preparatory sketches—relying solely on her feel for the place, the light, the view outside, and the ambiance she wants to create in the space. She relishes the large scale of painting entire rooms, the freedom that it gives her. The irrepressible energy of her personality comes through in every brushstroke and every flower arrangement she creates daily.

"I live permanently in this mix of rustic and sophistication. The grandeur of the place stimulates my imagination, but my eyes remain fixed, with great intensity and immense love, on the tiny plants on the ground—so small and so fragile." The line separating the inside and the outside is exuberantly obliterated, and, like the frescoes in Pompeii, Château de Beauvoir's wall paintings reflect a deep pleasure and delight in the natural world. As she sits in her dining room, where massive branches clamber up the ceiling and vases of buttercups mingle with their painted versions on the wall, Claire exclaims with her infectious laugh, "I love eating in here. It's like eating in a forest." Spoken like a woman in her true element.

Wondrous Flora

CARMEN ALMON   *Bordeaux & Payrac, France*

dogs teeth with

...enth century; by
...were also being

...ble White Daffodill.
...85(a), pp. 40–1, col.

THROUGHOUT HISTORY the recording of plant life has taken on many guises. The century between the mid-1700s and the mid-1800s was the golden age of botanical art in Europe, spurred by plant explorations in the East and the New World. Artists were called upon to record the exotic flora discovered from far-flung places, and their best botanical illustrations and floral still-lifes reflect the excitement and fascination of seeing these specimens for the first time. Nowhere is this more evident than in the work of Georg Dionysius Ehret, whose paintings of plants and flowers vibrate with life in their scientific precision and poetic expression. Inspired by Ehret's work, as well as that of Alexander Marshal, Basilius Besler, and Mark Catesby, Carmen Almon sculpts delicate botanical specimens that belie their materials: metal and enamel paint. A double anemone with a mass of frilly petals and a tangle of roots bends under the weight of its heavy bloom, as if it had jumped off the pages of the famous *Karlsruher Tulpenbuch*, the extraordinary collection of flower paintings that records the botanical treasures in the baroque gardens of the Margrave Karl Wilhehm's castle in Southwest Germany. A red poppy looks wind-blown next to tiny wildflowers, seemingly plucked from the field.

Following in the long tradition of botanical art, Carmen's compositions, while not exact replicas of nature, are naturalistically detailed, each flower identifiable and unique at the same time. Like an alchemist working solely with metal and paint, she brings her beloved eighteenth-century botanical illustrations to life by rendering them in the third dimension, imbued with her own thoughtful observations of nature. Being the daughter of a Spanish mother and an American diplomat meant a peripatetic childhood, with the family moving constantly to foreign lands. Carmen became adept at observing and watching everything in each new country, her curiosity making her a natural artist. She discovered the secret world of plants at the age of fourteen, when she was given her first pair of glasses. "I spent a week face down in the grass on the grounds of my school in Barcelona, completely amazed, observing all the plants and insects," recalls Carmen. What fascinates her most is the morphology of plants stemming from each one's uniquely evolved system of growth. "It's the same principle for all plants," explains Carmen, "the leaves are like solar panels and they find the best way to get to the sun, and the flowers ensure the plant's survival into the next generation by attracting insects to help them reproduce." These fundamental life-sustaining goals result in a bewildering multitude of forms and colors that enthrall all plant lovers. Today she spends much of her time studying the buzzing life among flowers, fruits, and insects in her own garden as well as those of friends in the Lot region of France. Even after all these years of observing nature, Carmen still retains her fascination and amazement at the richness of the botanical world, looking at each plant as if she had never seen it before.

Having devoted so much time registering the minutiae of plant life, Carmen is meticulous in her depiction of them. She sculpts her plants from copper and brass, letting accidents happen to give each one of her botanical tôles the quirkiness that "expresses the haphazardness of life." Splattered paint becomes marks on a leaf, showing "that the plant has had a history—damages, brown spots, like people's wrinkles and scars." Every petal and leaf is painstakingly cut from sheets of copper, using an assortment of nail scissors, pliers, and a jeweler's vise, then scored and shaped in Carmen's expert hands to take its form, be it a delicate pear blossom or a blowsy oriental poppy. Branches, leaves, and flowers are then soldered together. Each sculpture is scrupulously composed to effect just the right balance of chaos and grace found in nature. Sometimes Carmen will tear apart a large plant if it looks too perfect, the flowers too regular, or somehow lacking in poetry.

"The last phase sometimes takes the longest: getting the painting right, and getting just the right insect to land in just the right place," explains Carmen. To get the painting right, she applies layers of color with washes of enamel and oil paint thinned with turpentine, capturing the subtle hues and variations in a single bloom of hollyhock or larkspur. Great care is also taken to achieve the right color green for her leaves. "There are all these greens in plants: some more intense, some lighter, which goes to yellow, some with a film of white that makes them look bluer," she points out as she prepares her many shades of green paint.

The entire process sometimes takes several months from beginning to end. The finishing touch comes when Carmen finds the right place on the plant for one of her colorful insects: a menagerie of painted butterflies, grasshoppers, beetles, and dragonflies whose presence gives the composition an added sense of narrative. Carmen's quietly glorious flora sculptures reflect a wondrous communion with nature, each piece embodying a moment in time, plucked from her imagination with dazzling verve.

SPOTTED

SPOTTED
CAMPANULA
PUNCTATA

SMILACINA

BLEEDING HEART

V
72 cm

BESIER

POLYGONATUM   CYCAMEN

BABY EGGPLANT

WYSTERIA

VIRGINIA
CREEPER

H

61 Parrot Tulip 'Le Perroquet rouge' (*Tulipa gesneriana* L.). Body-colour on vellum, signed

Perroquet rouge

Plate 62
MAGNOLIA LILIIFLORA
Lily Magnolia
M. Schmutzer, watercolour, body-colour, ink on paper
Picture Archive, Austrian National Li...

Tafel 62
MAGNOLIA LILIIFLORA L.
Purpur-Magnolie
M. Schmutzer, Wasserfarben, Deckfarben, Tusche auf P...
Wien, Österreichische Nationalbibli...

Garden-to-Wall Flowers

OBERTO GILI *Bra, Italy*

WHEN HE IS NOT TRAVELING THE WORLD photographing glamorous people and places, photographer Oberto Gili retreats to *Il Picot*—the Peak, in Piedmontese—his bucolic home on the hillside of the northern Italian town of Bra. It is in these Piedmontese hills that Oberto spent his childhood summers, learning to grow flowers and vegetables and to tend animals from the local farmers. At an early age he wanted to be a farmer, but he went on to study mathematics and physics instead. While at university, he was given an enlarger and built his first darkroom. Antonioni's film *Blow Up*, with its depiction of a fashion photographer in swinging 60s London, inspired him to pursue photography professionally. By the 1980s he was living in New York and traveling around the world to shoot for glossy magazines. "JFK airport became my second home," he recalls. Fifteen years ago, Oberto decided to build his house in Bra, where his mother and brother both live nearby. For this jet-setting photographer, home is "a model of your life," and *Il Picot* is a compelling study of the accumulated experiences, friendships, and passions of his life. Here he is all the things he wants to be: farmer, gardener, photographer, artist, and chef.

Oberto shares *Il Picot* with his fiancée, Joy Sohn, and a menagerie of animals. It is as much a working farm as one man's Garden of Eden. "I do the vegetable gardens, I milk the cows, and I do the cheese, the butter, the bread—a very peasant life," says Oberto. A peasant life, perhaps, but one that makes ample room for art, literature, and beauty—"the guiding principle at *Il Picot*" being "aesthetic."

Lush semiformal gardens with fruit trees, grapevines, and flowers surround the many buildings on the farm. An experienced gardener with discerning taste (*Rosa roxburghii* is a favorite plant), Oberto is on a "never-ending search for new varieties of roses, irises, peonies, vegetables, and fruit trees." In early spring ravishing tree peonies and roses bloom in clouds of pink and red, while heavy trusses of lavender-colored wisterias drip from the walls, gates, and doorways. In summer, tall hollyhocks stained in shades from the palest blush to dark red wine dazzle from every corner of the garden. Grapevines snake up the walls to wrap themselves around balconies, offering clusters of grapes that hang tantalizingly within reach outside bedroom windows. Nasturtiums spill over terra cotta pots, and the scent of jasmine mixed with rosemary and lavender wafts in the breeze. Like all gardeners, Oberto plants flowers for the pleasure of watching them grow. He also loves to fill the house with his own arrangements. "I never use florist flowers," he proudly insists, finding them uninteresting. Instead, he pairs an unusual vase in the shape of a swan with the branches of fig leaves from an overgrown tree he just pruned. In the living room, Oberto's arrangement of spiky cardoon flowers echoes a painting of the same blooms by Cecil Beaton.

The flowers from the garden also serve as subjects for Oberto's photographic experiments. He captures their mysterious poses, in various stages of life and decay, often with a large-format camera. On sunny days, a large table is wheeled outside the studio to make prints by using sunlight exposure. Oberto constantly experiments with alternative printing methods, having a particular preference for gum and salt prints. His "garden-to-wall" flower prints are an ongoing project that neatly tie together his passions for gardening, flowers, and photography.

His endless search for new botanical beauties and photographic processes—an experiment with printing on metal is in the works—reflects Oberto's relentless curiosity. Alongside his many books on art and literature are great treatises on gardening and esoteric volumes on peonies and other flowers. He has also spent much time photographing other people's gardens. His own books include an evocative tome on eighteen of the world's most-loved city parks.

At *Il Picot*, the many strands of Oberto's abundantly rich life come together beautifully in a private Eden that is self-contained and bountiful. To others the desire to be a flower-loving farmer and a high-flying photographer at the same time might seem contradictory, but he has managed just that, weaving all his passions together in one extraordinarily beautiful place. He has created a garden that gives him all the earthy pleasures nature can yield. He grows flowers for his photographic studies. He rises at dawn to take the cows to the field, cooks every meal with the cornucopia harvested from his vegetable garden, and makes the best-tasting grappa from quince and other fruits on the farm. But most important of all, he generously shares this bounty with the people he loves: his friends and family.

Vessels & Flowers

FRANCES PALMER *Weston, Connecticut*

WHEN FRANCES PALMER MOVED OUT OF NEW YORK CITY to raise her family, she became interested in pottery because it enabled her to combine her love of cooking, gardening, and flowers. Inspired by Vanessa Bell and her creative output at Charleston Farmhouse, Frances wanted to make her own ceramics in which to serve food and to display the flowers that she grew herself. Fueled by the simple desire to set the table with her own creations, she became a self-taught potter whose work has been featured in the pages of *Vogue* and *World of Interiors*.

Today Frances works in a light-filled studio built within the frame of a 1790 house set on the grounds of her home in Connecticut. A couple of wheels and a kiln are installed on the studio's ground floor, while the finished works are displayed on the second floor, along with her vast collection of art books. Outside the studio is her flower garden, in which she grows the blossoms that keep her vases filled through the seasons. Fritillaries, daffodils, and tulips in early spring give way to a succession of peonies, bearded irises, poppies, and lilies, until amaranth, zinnia, and sunflowers take over by August. But the star of her garden is the dahlia, of which Frances grows about three hundred varieties. A photograph of the flower first sparked her intrigue, and a visit to the San Francisco Botanical Garden, with its extensive collection of the Mexican native flower, gave her an insight into the amazing varieties of dahlias. She particularly fell for the dramatic black-red dahlias, which she sought out from growers everywhere. Soon she added varieties in shades of pink and white, and eventually yellow. Along the way, other dahlia collectors began to entrust her with old and rare varieties, many from long-forgotten gardens. To Frances, flowers are "unspeakably beautiful," each one an "extraordinary miracle," but she finds the geometry of the dahlia's petals especially bewitching. The enormous variety in color and size, from tiny blooms of just one inch to those the size of dinner plates, adds to their appeal. Best of all, dahlias bloom from mid-summer until frost, making them the glorious finale of the growing season.

The garden and studio are intertwined, and Frances spends her time going from one to the other. A day typically begins at dawn in the garden, with Frances tending the plants before she heads into the studio. In between throwing and glazing sessions, she wanders back to the garden, losing herself among the flowers, which she cuts to arrange and photograph back in the studio. She also casts her favorite flowers in ceramic to embellish her vases and dishes. Even though flowers form the basis of her work, Frances grows them chiefly to indulge her passion for beautiful blossoms, or as she puts it, "I grow flowers just to be with them, and I make my vases to honor them." Every flower with its particular features inspires a different response in her work with the clay. For peonies, Frances makes a short and wide shape with a large opening to accommodate the generous blowsy blooms. Bud vases with the tiniest openings are for the delicate stems of fritillaries or grape hyacinths. For dahlias, she makes vases in taller, more dramatic shapes, often in celadon, the pale green complementing her favorite vibrant red varieties. "I can throw a vase every day of my life and still come up with something different each time," explains Frances, "because of the limitless possibilities that come from the garden." Trained as an art historian, she also finds inspiration in the ancient art of the Etruscan and Cycladic civilizations. She finds the most ancient shapes to be the most modern, which proved a perfect starting point for a collaboration with florist Emily Thompson. To create the perfect vessels for Emily's wildly sculptural arrangements, Frances came up with a series of Grecian urns, footed vases, and pitchers that reference seventeenth-century Dutch still-life paintings, all dramatically glazed with splashes of gold and palladium luster.

While Frances enjoys such symbiotic collaborations with other artists who share her love of flowers, she is happiest creating her work in the garden and the studio. As she points out, there is a parallel between growing flowers and making pots. In either process, you start with an idea in your mind, but to get to the end, whether it's a flower from a seed or a pot from a lump of clay, "you have to step back at some point and let that creation do its thing." A flower will never bloom the same way every time. Just as many factors—weather, soil conditions, etc.—can affect the outcome of a flower, the clay has to go through so many stages before it becomes the finished product. The results are never quite the same, either in flowers or pots, and so Frances will never tire of looking at her flowers or making pots to display them.

Wild Flowers

MARTYN THOMPSON & DOVE DRURY HORNBUCKLE

New York, New York

FROM THEIR LOFT IN SOHO, Martyn Thompson and Dove Drury Hornbuckle observe the horde of tourists and shoppers weaving in and out of the busy streets, moving in a blur of colors that, through their artistic eyes, resembles the flow and fluidity of a wild flower garden. And "what is more beautiful than flowers rustling in the wind," asks Dove, the conceptual mind behind the creative duo. Their home, perched above the crowded streets of New York's busiest shopping area, is a hive of creativity, a laboratory for their prolific artistic experiments. The spacious open-plan loft can barely contain their exuberant embrace of the "cliché medium" of flowers.

Martyn, whose mother is English, recalls happy childhood memories in his grandmother's wild English garden, where flowers held his fascination, especially pansies. When Dove was growing up in the country outside of New York, his mother, a classically trained dancer with a green thumb, filled the house with blooms that he loved to draw. Both men are attracted to the wildness of flowers, the "joy of chaos," as they see it. Martyn finds flowers full of surprises and energy, best appreciated when they are free to blow in the wind. Dove connects their effervescence with dance, referencing the late Butoh dancer Kazuo Ohno's idea of a blooming flower as a metaphor for a dance.

The uninhibited joy that Martyn and Dove find in flowers is given full expression in the home they share. Gigantic and colorful blooms in dripping paint explode across the living room wall like dancers leaping across the room. Inspired by Martyn's "earthy and sensual" process of working, Dove painted the mural in a literal burst of energy, trusting the broad gesture to give way to emotional expression. With such a bold and euphoric backdrop, the loft positively hums with a creative vibe. Dove's ceramic pieces are piled on the floor, waiting to be assembled into the Zodiac sign that Martyn photographs each month for his newsletter. The kitchen walls are covered with chalkboard paint, allowing Dove free rein to doodle. The drawings come and go, new images replacing old ones to give expression to changing moods. Fresh flowers spill over the coffee table, while an old bouquet of blooms past their prime rests on the table in Martyn's studio, ready for a close-up. While each has his own particular vision—Martyn approaches his work intuitively while Dove is more analytical—Martyn thinks that they inhabit "similar aesthetic planes," which allows them to collaborate and live in perfect harmony. They also inspire and complement each other.

At the beginning of their relationship, Martyn began a photographic series entitled "Falling in Love at the Institute," using artificial flowers to create painterly still-life tableaux in his signature evocative style. As an image-maker, Martyn is interested essentially in the colors and shapes of flowers and their cultural meanings. In his photographs, real flowers in all stages of life and death, as well as their artificial counterparts, are rendered in equally exquisite compositions. Martyn had the images printed to look more like paintings than photographs, using an alternative digital printing method. In an exploration to take his images beyond the boundaries of photography, Martyn began to experiment with printing the images on fabrics. This led to another series of floral still-lifes called "Cézanne's Shadow," the images of which he had transformed into intricate tapestries. The results are a modern take on an old craft, visually akin to pointillist paintings as much as traditional tapestries. He found that the tapestries worked well not only as wall hangings but also as cushion covers. Having begun his career as a fashion designer, Martyn became a photographer by taking pictures of his clothes, and he relished the idea of coming full circle to making fabrics with his photographs. Before long he had a full range of textiles for home furnishings, incorporating his beautiful botanical photographs. He and Dove also collaborated on a series of lamps, using his fabrics for the shade and Dove's ceramic pieces for the base.

Alarmed by "what we appear to be doing to the Earth," Martyn began another photographic series using artificial flowers, this time obliterating their colors with black paint and arranging them in ornate antique Capo-di-Monte vases spray painted black by a friend. Entitled "In Memoriam," the series evokes a sense of mourning, "an incredible sadness" that Martyn feels about the destruction of the environment. Dove sees the black paint over the flowers as a mark of man's destruction of something organic, like an oil spill over the ocean. Despite their fear that the human race is killing nature, Martyn and Dove are hopeful for their future, which holds the promise of a house in the country with a wild garden of their own. For Martyn, flowers will always remain an essential part of his work, for they remind him of the beauty inherent in the cycle of life, from birth to death and decay.

Patterns of Beauty

NEISHA CROSLAND   *London, England*

THE ROMANS WERE CITY DWELLERS who considered life in the countryside, with its lack of cultural activities, utterly boring. Instead, they preferred to plant gardens and paint bucolic scenes in their town houses to satisfy any longing for nature. Neisha Crosland completely relates to this lifestyle choice of the Romans. She lives and works in a bustling part of London, in a house that wraps itself around a central garden planted with a beautiful and varied collection of trees. Six clipped holm oaks make a small avenue on the lawn, while graceful olive trees, a colorful Eastern redbud, an espaliered Persian ironwood, and a wonderful gnarled Chinese Kiwi provide points of interest throughout the garden. Climbing roses, clematis, and grapevines clamber over walls, trailing across balconies and framing windows. Jasmine vines smother the old brick walls, maintaining a lush, green enclosure for the garden all year round. Alliums, tulips, irises, hellebores, and an ever-changing selection of annuals keep the garden in flowers most of the year.

This luxuriant garden, with its seasonal tableaux of plants and flowers, provides the daily backdrop for both Neisha's home and studio. Her lifelong love of flowers and plants began at an early age. "The world surrounds us with patterns, and there are many things on offer to influence and inspire, but on reflection, the things that made an impression on me when I was a child hold an influence on me still," says Neisha. "As a child, I remember seeing a Fritillaria in a flower bed and I was intrigued by the little delicate checks that decorated its petals. It seemed as if an elf or a faerie had come along overnight and painted them on. I then noticed that my stepfather had a pair of drawings of the same plants that were designs for Derby Porcelain plates." The use of floral motifs on everyday objects was a lesson that stayed with Neisha, who spent much of her childhood collecting flowers, pressing them, and drawing them with a fine Rotring pen nib to capture the intricate botanical details. Being myopic, she had "fantastic close-up vision" that "magnifies details like veins and variegated edges on a leaf, or the markings on a petal and hairs on a stem." These details, which she found exquisite and very touching, would later play a big part in the beautiful patterns she designs for wallpapers, fabrics, and rugs. "I seek to create designs with a symmetry and flow that can be likened to the geometric construction occurring within nature," she explains. Another lasting influence from childhood is a gift from her grandfather, an old edition of the *Complete Herbal* by the seventeenth-century English botanist and physician Nicholas Culpeper, with hundreds of illustrations of herbs and flowers that Neisha loved and copied meticulously. One of her favorite wallpaper designs, with life-size flowers reminiscent of both the book's illustrations and Mughal flower paintings and carvings, is named after Culpeper.

Having traveled extensively to Japan, India, Morocco, and much of Europe and America, Neisha finds inspiration in everything—from sixteenth-century Japanese kimonos with their minimalist renditions of flowers and leaves delicately embroidered with silver inlay, to Ottoman Empire textiles, the Moorish decoration of Alhambra, and the art of Matisse, Picasso, and Georgia O'Keeffe. Her studio and home reflect her wide interest in art and nature. Like the Romans who decorated their city dwellings with wall paintings, Neisha has the walls of her house painted with flowers, but in the style of nineteenth-century chinoiserie. In the entrance hall that doubles as a garden room, painted flowering branches and bamboo stalks bend gracefully against a pale blue background, the work of the artist Rosie Nemem, who also painted a blue and white floral floor in a hallway upstairs. In the drawing room, on a wall with an oval window that frames the view of the garden, another artist, Ian Harper, painted cherry blossoms on a gold-leaf background, bringing the garden and interior closer together. Another weeping cherry blossom tree against a gold background decorates the dining room.

In the studio, piles of sketchbooks demonstrate Neisha's keen eye for patterns and her deep appreciation of the details in nature, the intricacies of flowers and foliage. An early painting of tulips has the gracefulness and delicate touch of an Ottoman textile pattern. Other floral and plant motifs are hand painted on silk to make wall coverings. A series of Daphne du Maurier's novels bears her signature abstracted floral patterns on the covers. But flowers and plants serve more than their decorative purposes. Back in the garden, Neisha also grows strawberries that her children love to eat and herbs that she uses to make tisane. In the midst of one of the largest and busiest cities in the world, Neisha has created an oasis steeped in nature, magnificently surrounded by the beauty of flowers, just as the Romans did over a thousand years ago.

MY COUSIN RACHEL
DAPHNE DU MAURIER

INTRODUCED BY
SALLY BEAUMAN

Acknowledgments

I HAVE ALWAYS BEEN PARTIAL TO FLOWERS and find the history of our botanical fascination very intriguing. I love how we incorporate the beauty of flowers into almost everything we do, and for this book I wanted to explore what it is about them that inspires different artists and designers. Claire Basler is the first artist I photographed for the book. I discovered her work online by chance and wrote to her. She very kindly wrote back and invited me to come and stay at Château de Beauvoir. I had the most magical visit with Claire and her partner, Pierre Imhoff, in the summer of 2014. It was the most felicitous start for the project. Claire and Pierre were such gracious and generous hosts that I felt at home immediately in their extraordinary château. It was like no other home I had ever seen, let alone had the pleasure of living in. Claire's flowers and paintings took over the entire place, blurring the line between the landscape and the house. I photographed all day long, and in the evening we gathered in the garden, watching flaming sunsets over the valley below, drinking champagne as the prerequisite aperitif before dinner. Claire and I spent every evening talking late into the night. By the time I left, I felt as if I had known her for a long time. I just couldn't believe how lucky I was.

What I couldn't have known then is that I would repeat virtually the same experience with the other subjects of the book. Carmen Almon, her husband, Thierry Job, and their daughter, Zoe, welcomed me to their apartment in Bordeaux and their country house in the Lot region with the same hospitality and generosity. Carmen took me to all of her friends' gardens around her country house, where she works for part of the year. The countryside during the month of May was spectacular. Fields of red poppies stretched out gloriously along the roads. The gardens I visited were bursting with fragrant roses, mock oranges, peonies, bearded irises, and other flowers. We spent many hours talking, on the long train ride from Bordeaux and over delicious meals on the terrace under vine-covered pergola at her country house. I came to appreciate her work so much more and saw the connection between her sculptures and the eighteenth-century botanical illustrations that inspired her.

Nothing prepared me for my encounter with Umberto Pasti and his partner, Stephan Janson. Umberto is an Italian writer who first came to Tangier thirty years ago and fell in love with the wildflowers there. His love of flowers is infectious, and the minute I stepped through the gate of his house in Tangier, a rich botanical world opened up for me. The house is built on a steep slope, and the garden unfolds in a series of lush and densely planted terraces that are intensely perfumed at night. Umberto introduced me to so many wonderful and unfamiliar (at least to me) plants that thrive in the mild climate of Tangier. He is also a passionate collector of Islamic tiles, so many of which are rich in floral imagery. I spent an entrancing, edifying week in Stephan and Umberto's lively company, immersed in the beauty of their floral world.

I had the most enchanting visit to Oberto Gili and Joy Sohn's home in Bra, Italy, where flowers bloomed in abundance both in the garden and on the walls. Oberto's prodigious talents as a gardener, cook, and photographer are especially enviable. Sarah Ryhanen and Eric Famisan welcomed me several times to their farm World's End, a place of uncommon beauty, where the emotional power of flowers is rendered palpable. Rachel and Alan Dein allowed me into their charming North London home to observe Rachel at work and to spend time with their family. Each encounter with the artists in this book has been equally rewarding in its own way. I learned to see flowers through the subjects' eyes, each one unique in its perspective. Neisha Crosland, being myopic, discerns patterns in flowers that she uses in her designs. Frances Palmer sees their myriad shapes and colors as cues for the shapes and colors of her vases. Martyn Thompson and Dove Drury Hornbuckle's flower-strewn universe is out of the ordinary, extravagant, and utterly inspiring. Livia Cetti revels in the complexity of each blossom that she renders in paper. Miranda Brooks taught me the pleasures of nurturing plants and the poetry of gardens. What all of the artists have in common is a profound connection to nature and the greatest possible delight in a gloriously flowery world. Without their extraordinary work, this book would simply not exist. I am enormously indebted to them for their inspiration and generosity.

My gratitude also goes Charles Miers, for allowing me to indulge in my floral obsession first with *Bringing Nature Home* and now this book; and Alexandra Tart, for her careful editing, belief in my vision, and patient guidance.

My friend Scot Schy was instrumental in making this book as beautiful and elegant as it is. He patiently and thoughtfully labored over the design as many times as necessary, often working remotely on late nights without complaint. Thanks also to Angela Taormina, who put in the finishing touches and diligently enabled us to deliver the book to the printer on time.

My warmest thanks to Dung Ngo, who advised me every step of the way in the long process of creating this book. To Deborah Needleman, I offer a heartfelt thank you for her unstinting support, friendship, and introduction to Umberto Pasti.

My friends lent a patient ear during the various stages of this book, and I am especially grateful to Véronique Gambier, Vanessa Holden, and Melissa Goldstein for their helpful input. I also owe a wholehearted thank you to my brother-in-law, Scott Crider, who read the many drafts of the introduction.

Finally, my deepest gratitude to Julian and Lily Wass, who make everything possible.

Page 3: **RAINER MARIA RILKE**,
*Letters of Rainer Maria Rilke 1892–
1910*, translated by Jane Bannard
Greene & M. D. Herter Norton,
W. W. Norton & Company, 1969.

Page 8: **JEAN RENOIR**, *Pierre-
Auguste Renoir, mon père*,
Gallimard, 1981.

Page 85: **UMBERTO PASTI & PIERRE
LE-TAN**, *Le Bonheur du Crapaud*,
Flammarion, 2015.

Page 212: 'Poem' drawings by
TEDDY MILLINGTON-DRAKE.

FIRST PUBLISHED
in the United States of America in 2016 by
Rizzoli International Publications, Inc.
300 Park Avenue South, New York, NY 10010
www.rizzoliusa.com

© 2016 by Ngoc Minh Ngo
Book Design by Scot Schy
Production Design by Angela Taormina

2016 2017 2018 2019 / 10 9 8 7 6 5 4 3 2 1

DISTRIBUTED
in the U.S. trade by Random House, New York

PRINTED IN CHINA

ISBN-13: 978-0-8478-4850-8

Library of Congress Control Number: 2016935444

PAPAVER RVBRVM
. *Flore per extremitates*
incifo.

MHR
PAPAVER HO

Ital. *Papa*
Gall. *Pav*
Germ. *Mo*
Belg. *Ho*

Dioſc. lib. 4. cap. 55.

Flore

papaver ſatiuum flore fimbriato   *1700*

euse' (*Primula* × *pubescens* Jacq.). Body-colour on vellum, signed, 17

Fille Amoureuse